The Spirit of Zoroastrianism

By Henry S. Olcott

Copyright © 2021 Lamp of Trismegistus. All rights reserved. No part of this publication may be reproduced or transmitted in any form or by any means, electronic or mechanical, including photocopying, recording, or by any information storage and retrieval system, without permission in writing from Lamp of Trismegistus. Reviewers may quote brief passages.

ISBN: 978-1-63118-564-9

Esoteric Classics

Other Books in this Series and Related Titles

Aurora of the Philosophers by Paracelsus (978-1-63118-507-6)

Clairvoyance and Psychic Abilities by A Besant &c (978-1-63118-403-1)

The Feminine Occult by various authors (978-1-63118-711-7)

Rosicrucian Rules, Secret Signs, Codes and Symbols by various (978-1-63118-488-8)

An Outline of Theosophy by C W Leadbeater (978-1-63118-452-9)

Paracelsus, the Four Elements and Their Spirits by M P Hall (978-1-63118-400-0)

The Stone of the Philosophers by A E Waite (978-1-63118-509-0)

The Eleusinian Mysteries and Rites by Dudley Wright (978–1–63118–530–4)

The Use of Evil by Annie Besant (978-1-63118-532-8)

The Alchemical Catechism of Paracelsus by Paracelsus (978-1-63118-513-7)

Alchemy in the Nineteenth Century by Helena P Blavatsky (978-1-63118-446-8)

Qabbalistic Teachings and the Tree of Life by M P Hall (978-1-63118-482-6)

The Devil in Love by Jacques Cazotte (978–1–63118–499–4)

The Hidden Mysteries of Christianity by Annie Besant (978–1–63118–534–2)

History, Analysis and Secret Tradition of the Tarot by Hall &c (978-1-63118-445-1)

Crystal Vision Through Crystal Gazing by Frater Achad (978-1-63118-455-0)

The Golden Verses of Pythagoras: Five Translations (978-1-63118-479-6)

The Historic, Mythic and Mystic Christ by Annie Besant (978-1-63118-533-5)

The Machinery of the Mind by Dion Fortune (978-1-63118-451-2)

The A E Waite Reader: A Selection of Occult Essays (978-1-63118-515-1)

The Leadbeater Reader: A Selection of Occult Essays (978-1-63118-483-3)

Audio versions are also available on Audible, Amazon and Apple

Other Books in this Series and Related Titles

The Brotherhood of Religions by Annie Besant (978-1-63118-563-2)

Fourth Book of Maccabees by Josephus (978-1-63118-562-5)

The Story of Ahikar by Ahiqar (978-1-63118-561-8)

Vision of the Spirit by C. Jinarajadasa (978-1-63118-560-1)

Occult Arts by William Q. Judge (978-1-63118-559-5)

Kali the Mother by Sister Nivedita (978-1-63118-558-8)

Love and Death by Sri Aurobindo (978-1-63118-557-1)

Times and Seasons Volume 1, Numbers 4-6 (978-1-63118-556-4)

Times and Seasons Volume 1, Numbers 1-3 (978-1-63118-555-7)

The Book of John Whitmer by John Whitmer (978-1-63118-554-0)

Interesting Account of Several Remarkable Visions (978-1-63118-553-3)

The Evening and Morning Star Volume 1, Numbers 11 & 12 (978-1-63118-552-6)

The Evening and Morning Star Volume 1, Numbers 1 & 2 (978-1-63118-547-2)

Private Diary of Joseph Smith 1832-1834 (978-1-63118-546-5)

An Address to All Believers in Christ Elder David Whitmer (978-1-63118-545-8)

A Manuscript on Far West by Reed Peck (978-1-63118-544-1)

The Story of Mormonism by James E Talmage (978-1-63118-543-4)

The Philosophy of Mormonism by James E Talmage (978-1-63118-542-7)

The Angel of the Prairies or A Dream of the Future (978-1-63118-541-0)

The Book of Abraham: Mormon History by George Reynolds (978-1-63118-540-3)

Pearl of Great Price by Joseph Smith (978-1-63118-539-7)

Audio versions are also available on Audible, Amazon and Apple

Table of Contents

Introduction...7

The Spirit of Zoroastrianism...9

INTRODUCTION

The word "esoteric" can be difficult to define. Esotericism in general can be seen less as a system of beliefs and more as a category, which encompasses numerous, different systems of beliefs. It's a bit of juxtaposition, since the word "esoteric" indicates something that few people know about, while the term itself broadly covers numerous philosophies, practices, areas of study and belief systems.

In a greater sense, Esotericism acts as a storehouse for secret knowledge, which is often considered ancient (by *tradition, if not by fact),* passed down from generation to generation, in private. At various times in history, simply possessing the knowledge of some of these subjects, was considered illegal and a jailable offence, if discovered. This usually included such general topics as Alchemy, Pharmacology, Qabalah, Hermeticism, Occultism, Ceremonial Magic, Astrology, Divination, Rosicrucianism and so on. Collectively, these areas of study were often referred to as the esoteric sciences.

Sometimes, the outer garment of a subject isn't esoteric, while what is hidden beneath it, is. As an example, Freemasonry isn't necessarily esoteric by nature (at *least not anymore),* but certain signs, passwords and handshakes given to the candidate during their initiation, are in fact, esoteric, in the sense that they are hidden from the general public.

Today, in the twenty-first century, such topics are readily available at bookstores across the country, and numerous mainsteam publishers offer beginners guides and coffee-table volumes on many of these subjects, intended for mass appeal. Books like *"The Secret"* have turned previously arcane topics into household knowledge. All that being the case, however, it isn't to say that there still aren't buried secrets to uncover, ancient wisdom being ignored and forgotten mysteries to be explored. In fact, it is often that we are only able to further our own studies by standing on the shoulders of these disappearing giants.

Lamp of Trismegistus is doing its part to help preserve humanity's esoteric history by making some of these classics available to those students who are seeking to unearth the knowledge of these ancient colossi.

So, be sure to check other titles from our *Esoteric Classics* series, as well as our *Occult Fiction, Theosophical Classics, Foundations of Freemasonry Series, Supernatural Fiction, Paranormal Research Series, Studies in Buddhism* and our *Christian Apocrypha Series*. You can also download the audio versions of most of these titles from Amazon, Apple or Audible, for learning on the go.

THE SPIRIT OF ZOROASTRIANISM

With great diffidence I have accepted your invitation to address the Parsis upon the theme of the present discourse. The subject is so noble, its literature so rich, its ramifications so numerous, that no living man could possibly do it full justice in a single lecture. Happy indeed, will I be, if I succeed in communicating to one or two of the learned Parsi scholars, who honor me with their presence, some of the deep interest which I have had for years in the esoteric meaning of the Mazdean faith. My hope is to attract your attention to the only line of research which can lead you towards the truth. That line was traced by Zoroaster and followed by the Magi, the Mobeds, and the Dasturs of old. Those great men have transmitted their thoughts to posterity under the safe cover of an external ritual. They have masked them under a symbolism and ceremonies that guard their mighty secrets from the prying curiosity of the vulgar crowd, but hide nothing from those who desire to know all. Do not misunderstand me. I am not pretending that I know all, or a fraction of all; at best I have had but a glimpse of the reality. But even that little is quite enough to convince me that, within the husk of your modern religion, there is the shining soul of the old faith that came to Zardusht in his Persian name, and once illuminated the whole trans- Himalayan world. You — children of Iran, heirs of the Chaldean lore ! you — who so loved your religion that neither the sword of Omar, nor the delights of home, nor the yearning of our common humanity to live among the memories of our ancestors, could make you deny that religion; you — who, for the sake of conscience, fled from your native land and erected an altar for the symbolical Sacred Fire in foreign countries, more hospitable than yours had become; you — men of intelligence, of an ancient character for probity, of enterprise in all good works— you alone can lift the dark veil of this modern Parsi-ism, and let the 'hidden splendor' again blaze forth. Mine is but the office of the friendly wayfarer who points you to the mouth of the private road that leads through your own domain. I am not, if you please, a man — only a VOICE. I need not even appeal to you to strip away the foreign excrescences that, during twelve centuries of residence among strangers, have fastened themselves upon primitive Zoroastrianism; nor recite to you its simple yet all-sufficient code of morality, and ask you to live up to it more closely. This work has already been undertaken by the intelligent and public-spirited members of your own community. But I am to show you that your religion is in agreement with the most recent discoveries of modern science, and that the freshest graduate from Elphinstone College has no cause to blush for the 'ignorance' of Zoroaster! And I am to prove to you that your faith rests upon the rock of truth, the living rock of occult science, upon which the initiated progenitors of mankind built every one of the religions that have since swayed the thoughts and stimulated the aspirations of a hundred generations of worshippers. Let others trace back the history of Zoroastrianism to and beyond the time of the Bactrian King, Vistasp; and reconcile the quarrels of Aristotle, Hermippus, Clement, Alexander Polyhistor and other ancient as well as modern critics, as to when Zoroaster lived and where was his birthplace: these are non-essentials. It is of far less moment to know where and of what parentage a religious reformer was born, than to be sure of what he taught and whether his teaching is calculated to bless mankind or not. Plotinus, the philosopher, so well knew this that he would not tell, even to Porphyry his pupil and literary biographer, what was his native country, what his real name, or his parentage. As regards Zoroaster two things are affirmed, *viz.,* that about six centuries B. C. one man of that name lived — whether or not several others preceded him, as several highly respectable authorities affirm is the fact; and that the religion he preached, whether old or new, was of so noble a character that it indelibly stamped its impress upon the then chief school of western philosophy, that of Greece. [In the oldest Iranian book called the *Desatir* — a collection of the teachings of the oldest Iranian prophets (to make the number fifteen and include among them Simkendesh, or 'Secander' is a grave error, as may be proved on the authority of Zoroaster himself in that book) — Zoroaster stands thirteenth in that list. The fact is significant. Respecting the period of Zoroaster the *first,* or his personality, there is no trustworthy information given by any of the western scholars; their authorities conflict in the most perplexing manner. Indeed among many discordant notices, I find the earliest Greek classic writers who tell us that Zoroaster lived from 600 to 5,000 years before the Trojan War, or 6,000 years before Plato. Again, it is declared by Berosus, the Chaldean priest, that Zoroaster was a founder of an Indian dynasty in Babylon, 2,200 B.C. while the later native traditions inform us that he was the son of Purushaspa, and a contemporary of Gustaspa, the father of Darius, which would bring him within 600 B. C. Lastly it is mentioned by Bunsen that he was born at Bactria before the emigration of the Bactrians to the Indus, which took place, as the learned Egyptologist tells us, 3,784 B. C.. Among this host of contradictions, what conclusion can one come to? Evidently, there is but one hypothesis left; and that is that they are all wrong, the reason for it being the one I find in the secret traditions of the esoteric doctrine — namely, that there were several teachers of that name. Neither Plato nor Aristotle, so accurate in their statements, is likely to have transformed 200 years into 6,000. As to the generally accepted native tradition, which makes the great prophet a contemporary of Darius' father it is absurd and wrong on the very face of it. Though the error is too palpable to need any elaborate confutation, I may say a few words in regard to it. The latest researches show that the Persian inscriptions point to Vistasp as the last of the line of Kaianian princes who ruled in Bactria, while the Assyrian conquest of that country took place in 1,200 B. C. Now this alone would prove that Zoroaster lived twelve or thirteen hundred years B. C., instead of the six hundred assigned to him: and thus that he could not have been a contemporary of Darius Hystaspes, whose father was so carelessly, and for such a length of time, confounded in this connection with Vistasp who nourished six centuries earlier. If we add to this the historical discrepancy between the statement of Ommianus Marcellinus, which makes Darius crush the Magi and introduce the worship of Ahuramazda, and the inscription on the tomb of that king which states that he was 'teacher and hierophant of Magianism': and that other no less significant and very important fact that the Zoroastrian *Avesta* shows no signs of the knowledge of its writer or writers of either the Medes, the Persians or the Assyrians — the ancient books of the Parsis remaining silent upon, and showing no acquaintance with, any of the nations that have been known to have dwelt in or near the western parts of Iran, — the accepted figure 600 B. C. as the period in which the prophet is alleged to have flourished becomes absolutely improbable.

It is therefore safe to come to the following conclusions: — (1) That there were several, in all *seven,* say the Secret Records, *Ohuruasters* or spiritual teachers of Ahuramazda, an office corrupted later into *Guru-asters* and *Zuru-asters* from *Zera-Ishtar,* the title of the Chaldean or Magian priests; and (2) that the last of them was Zoroaster of the *Desatir,* the thirteenth of the prophets, and the seventh of that name. It was he who was the contemporary of Vistasp, the last of the Kaianian princes, and the Compiler of Vendidad, the Commentaries upon which are lost, there remaining now but the dead letter. Some of the facts given in the Secret Records, though to the exact scholar merely traditional, are very interesting. They are to the effect that there exists a certain hollow rock fall of tablets in a gigantic cave bearing the name of the first Zoroaster under his Magian appellation, and that the tablets may yet be rescued some day. This cave, with its rocks and tablets and its many inscriptions on the walls, is situated at the summit of one of the peaks of the Thian Shan Mountains, far beyond their junction with the Belor Tagh, somewhere along their eastern course. One of the half-pictorial and half-written prophecies and teachings attributed to Zoroaster himself relates to that deluge which has transformed an inland sea into the dreary desert called Shamo or Gobi Desert. The esoteric key to the mysterious creeds, flippantly called at one time the Sabian or Planetary Religion, at another, the Solar or Fire-Worship, "hangs in that cave", says the legend. In it the great Prophet is represented with a golden star on his heart and as belonging to that race of antediluvian giants mentioned in the sacred books of the Chaldeans and of the Jews. It matters little whether this information is accepted or rejected. Since the rejection of it would not make the other hypothesis more trustworthy, it may just as well be mentioned here.

It is also, as I believe, certain that this man was an Initiate in the sacred mysteries, or – to put it differently — that he had, by a certain course of mystical study, penetrated all the hidden mysteries of man's nature and of the world about him. Zoroaster is by the Greek writers often called the Assyrian 'Nazaret'. This term comes from the word *Nazar*, or *Nazir* — set apart, separated. The Nazars were a sect of Adepts, very ancient, existing ages before Christ. They are described as "physicians, healers of the sick by the imposition of the hands", and as initiated into the Mysteries (see treatise *Nazir* in the Talmud). The Jews, returning from the Babylonian captivity, were thoroughly imbued with Zoroastrian and Magian ideas; their forefathers had agreed with the Sabians in the Bactric worship, the adoration of the Sun, Moon, and five Planets, the SABBAOTH and

Realm of Light. In Babylon they had learned to worship the Seven-Rayed God. And so we find running throughout the Christian as well as the Jewish Scriptures, the septenary system, which culminates in the *Book of Revelation,* the final pamphlet of the Bible, in the Heptaktis; and a prophecy of the coming of the Persian Sosiosh under the symbol of the Christian Messiah, riding, like the former, upon a white horse. By the Jewish sect of the Pharisees, whose great teacher was Hillel, the whole angelology and symbolism of the Zoroastrians were accepted, and infused into Jewish thought: and their Hebrew Kabalah or secret book of occult wisdom, was the offspring of the Chaldean Kabalah. This deathless work is the receptacle of all the ancient lore of Chaldea, Persia, Media, Bactria, and of the pre-Iranian period. The name by which its students in the secret lodges of the Jewish Pharisees, or Pharsis, were known was *Kabirim* — from *Kabiri,* the Mystery Gods of Assyria. *Zoroastrianism* and *Magianism* proper were, then, the chief source of both esoteric Judaism and esoteric Christianity. But not only has this subtle spirit left the latter religion, under the pressure of worldliness and skeptical enquiry: it also long ago left Judaism. The modern Hebrews are not Kabalists but Talmudists, holding to the latter interpretations of the Mosaic canon; only here and there can we now find a real Kabalist, who knows the true religion of his people and whence it was derived.

The real history of Zoroaster and his religion has never been written. The Parsis have lost the key, as the Jews and Christians have lost that of their respective faiths, and as I find the Southern Buddhists have also. Not to the living pandits or priests of either of those religions can the laity look for light. They can only quote the opinions of ancient Greek and Roman, or modern German, French or English writers. Today nearly all that your most enlightened scholars know about your religion is what they have collated from

European sources, and that is almost exclusively about its literature and external forms. And see what ridiculous mistakes some of those authorities make at times!

The Rev. Dr. Prideaux, treating of the *Sad-dar,* says that Zoroaster preached incest! — that "nothing of this nature is unlawful, a man may *not only marry his sister or daughter, but even his mother* !" [Ancient Universal History, iv 206] He quotes no Zend authority, nothing written by a Parsi, but only Jewish and Christian authorities, such as Philo, Tertullian, and Clement Alexandrinus. Eutychius, a priest and archimandrite at Constantinople, writes, in the fifth century, on Zoroastrianism as follows: "Nimrod beheld a fire rising out of the earth and he worshipped it, and from that time the Magi worshipped fire. And he appointed a man named Andeshan to be the priest and servant of the Fire. The Devil, shortly after that, spoke out of the midst of the fire, as did Jehovah to Moses, saying: 'No man can serve the Fire or learn Truth in my Religion, unless first he shall commit incest with his mother, sister and daughter! He *did as he was commanded,* and from that time the priests of the Magians practiced incest: but Andeshan was the first inventor of that doctrine". I quote this as a sample of the wretched stuff that has been written against the Zoroastrian religion by its enemies. The above words are simply the dead- letter mistranslation of the secret doctrine, of which portions are to be found in certain old rare MSS. possessed by the Armenians at Etchmiadzine, the oldest monastery in the Russian Caucasus. They are known as the Mesrobian MSS. Should the Bombay Parsis show any real general interest in the rehabilitation of their religion, I think I may promise them the unpaid but, all the same, friendly assistance of Madame Blavatsky, whose friend of thirty-seven years standing, the Prince Dondoukoff Korsakoff, has just notified her of his appointment by His Majesty the Czar, as Viceroy of the Caucasus.

In one of such old MSS, then, it is said of the Initiate, or Magus: "He who would penetrate the secrets of (sacred) Fire and unite with it, as the Yogi 'unites himself with the Universal Soul', must first unite himself, soul and body, to the Earth his *mother*, to Humanity his *sister*, and to Science his *daughter.*" Quite a different thing, you perceive, from the abhorrent precept ascribed to the Founder of your Mazdean faith. And this example should serve as a warning to your so-called educated youth against turning up his classical nose at his ancestral religion as 'unscientific' and nonsensical.

A curious and sad thing, indeed, it is to see how completely the old life has gone out of Zoroastrianism. Originally a highly spiritual faith — I know of none more so — and represented by Sages and Adepts of the highest rank among Initiates, it has shrunk into a purely exoteric creed full of ritualistic practices not understood, taught by a numerous body of priests as a rule ignorant of the first elements of spiritual philosophy, and represented in prayers of which not one has a meaning to those who recite them daily — the shriveled shell that once held a radiant soul. Yet all that Zoroastrianism ever was it might be made again. The light still shines, though in darkness, enclosed in the clay vessel of materialism. Whose shall be the holy hand to break the jar of clay and let the hidden glory be seen? Where is the Mobed who shall in our day and generation rise to the ancient dignity of his profession, and redeem it from degradation? Not before he learns the true meaning of his own name, and strives once more to become worthy of it, can he be found. How many among the modern priests know that their title of *Mobed* or *Mogbed* comes from *Mag*, a word used by the prophet Jeremiah to designate a Babylonian Initiate, which, in its turn, is an abbreviation of Maginsiah — the great and wise? 'Maghistom' was once the title of Zoroaster's highest disciples, and the synonym of wisdom. Speaking of them Cicero says: *Sapientium et doctorum genus majorum habebatur in Persis* (The wise and learned class of the Magians live among the Persians) a degradation so great as to oblige even a Parsi author [The *Parsis,* p 277. Mr. Dosabhai Framji.] to say that they recite parrot-like all the chapters requiring to be repeated on occasions of religious ceremonies? .. "Ignorant and unlearned as these priests are, they do not and cannot command the respect of the laity. . . the position of the 'so- called' spiritual guides has fallen into contempt" he adds, also, some priests "have given up a profession which has ceased to be honorable and . . become contractors for constructing railroads in the Bombay Presidency". Some of the present Dasturs "are intelligent and well-informed men, possessing a considerable knowledge of their religion; but the mass of the priesthood are profoundly ignorant of its first principles".[Ibid, p 279]

I ask you, men of practical sense, what is the certain fate of a religion that has descended so low, that its priests are regarded by the Behedin (laity) as fit only to be employed in menial services, such as bringing things to you from the bazaar, and doing household tasks? What is it? I put it to you. Do you suppose that such a dried corpse will be left long above ground by the fresh and critical minds you are educating at college? Nay, do you not see how they are already treating it: how they abstain from visiting your temples: how sullenly they 'make kusti, and go through their other daily ceremonies: how they avoid, as much as possible, every attention to the prescribed ordinances: how they are gathering in clubs to drink pegs and play cards: how they are defiling themselves by evil associations, smoking in secret, some even openly, and prating glibly the most skeptical sophistries they have read in European books, written by deluded modern theorists? Yes, — he cloud gathers over the fire-altar, the once fragrant wood of truth is wet with the deadly dews of doubt, a pestilential vapor fills the Atash-Behram, and unless some Regenerator is raised up among you, the name of Zoroaster may, before many generations, be known only as that of the Founder of an extinct Faith.

In his preface to the translation of the *Vendidad,* the learned Dr. Darmesteter says: " he Key to the Avesta is not the Pahlavi, but the Veda. The Avesta and the Veda are two echoes of one and the same voice, the reflex of one and the same thought: the Vedas, therefore, are both the best lexicon and the "best commentary to the Avesta", [The *Sacred Books of the East,* edited by Professor F. Max Müller Vol IV, P 26] This he defines as the extreme view of the Vedic scholars, and while, personally, he does not subscribe to them entirely, he yet holds that we cannot perfectly comprehend the Avesta without utilizing the discoveries of the Vedic pandits. But neither Darmesteter, nor Anquetil Duperron, nor Haug, nor Spiegel, nor Sir William Jones, nor Rapp (whose work has been so perfectly translated into English by your eminent Parsi scholar Mr. K. R. Kama), nor Koth, nor any philological critic whose works I have read, has named the true key to Zoroaster's doctrine. For it, we must not search among the dry bones of words. No, it hangs within the door of the Kabalah — the Chaldean secret volume, where, under the mask of symbols and misleading phrases, it is kept for the use of the true searcher after arcane knowledge. The entire system of ceremonial purifications, which in itself is so perfect that a modern Parsi, a friend of mine, has remarked that Zoroaster was the best of Health Officers, is, it seems to me, typical of the moral purification required of him who would either, while living, attain the Magian's knowledge of hidden laws of nature and his power to wield them for good purposes, or, after a well ordered life, attain by degrees to the stage of spiritual beatitude, called Moksha by the Hindus and Nirvana by the Buddhists. The defilements by touch of various objects that you are warned against, are not visible defilements, like that of the person by contact with filth, but psychic defilements, through the influence of their bad magnetic aura — a subtle influence proceeding from certain living organisms and inert substances — which is antipathetic to development as an adept. If you will compare your books with the *Yoga Sutras* of the Hindus, and the *Tripitikas* of the Buddhists, you will see that each exact for the student and practitioner of occult science, a place, an atmosphere, and surroundings that are perfectly pure. Thus the Magus, or Yozdathraigar, the Yogi, and the Arhat all retire, either to the innermost or topmost chambers of a temple, where no stranger is permitted to enter, bringing his impure magnetism with him, or to the heart of a forest, a secluded cave, or a mountain height. In the tower of Belus at Babylon, virgin seeresses gazed into magical mirrors and aerolites, to see their prophetic visions: the yogi retires to his subterranean *gupha,* or to jungle fastnesses: and the Chinese books tell us that the 'great Nachus' of their sacred doctrine dwell in the snowy range of the Himavat. The books alleged to have been inspired by God, or delivered by His angels to man, have always, I believe, been delivered on mountains. Zoroaster got the Avesta on Ushidarina, a mountain by the river Daraga; [Venidad, xIix] Moses received the tables of the Law on Mount Sinai; [Exodus, xxxiv] Muhammmed was given the Koran on Mount Hara; [Am. Cyc, Vol, xi, 612] and the Hindu Rshis lived in the Himalayas. Sakya Muni left no inspired books, but, although he received the illumination of the Buddha-hood in the plains, under a Bo-tree, he had prepared himself by years of austerities in the mountains near Rajagriha. The obstructive power of foul human, animal, vegetable, and even mineral auras, or magnetisms, has always been understood by occult students, from the remotest times. This is the true reason why none but initiated and consecrated priests have ever been allowed to step within the precincts of the holiest places. The custom is not at all the offspring of any feeling of selfish exclusiveness, but is based upon known psycho - physiological laws. Even the modern Mesmerists and Spiritualists know this: and the latter, at least, carefully avoid 'mixing magnetisms', which always hurt a sensitive subject. All nature is a compound of conflicting, hence counterbalancing and equilibrating forces. Without this there could be no such thing as stability. Is it not the contest of centrifugal and centripetal attractions that keeps our earth and every other orb of heaven revolving in its orbit? The law of the universe is a distinct dualism while the creative energy is at work, and of a compound unism when at rest. And the personification of these opposing powers by Zoroaster was but the perfectly scientific and philosophical statement of a profound truth. The secret laws of this war of forces are taught in the Chaldean Kabalah. Every neophyte who sets himself to study for Initiation is taught these secrets, and he is made to prove them by his own experiments, step by step, as his powers and knowledge increase. Zoroastrianism has two sides — the open, or patent, and the concealed, or secret. Born of the mind of a Bactrian seer, it partakes of the nature of the primitive Iranian national religion and of the new spirituality that was poured into it, from the Source of all Truth, through the superb lens of Zoroaster's mind.

The Pàrsis have been charged with being worshippers of the visible fire. This is wholly false. They face the fire, as they also face the sun and the sea, because in them they picture to themselves the hidden Light of Lights, Source of all Life, to which they give the name of Ormazd. How well and how beautifully is this expressed in the writings of Robert Mudd, the English Mystic of the seventeenth century: [See Hargrave Jennings. *The Rosicrucians,* p. 69]

Regard Fire, then with other eyes than with those soulless incurious ones with which thou hast looked upon it as the most ordinary thing. Thou hast forgotten what it is — or rather thou hast never known. Chemists are silent about it ... Philosophers talk of it as anatomists discourse of the constitution, or the parts, of the human body. ... It is made for man and this world, and it is greatly like him — that is mean, they would add . . . But is this all? Is this the sum of that casketed lamp of the human body? — thine own body, thou unthinking world's machine — thou man? Or, in the fabric of this clay lamp (What a beautiful simile) burneth there not a Light? Describe that, ye doctors of physics!. . . Note the goings of the Fire. . . Think that this thing is bound up in matter chains. Think that He is outside of all things: and that thou and thy world are only the thing-between: and that outside and inside are both identical, couldst thou understand the supernatural truths! Reverence Fire, for its meaning, and tremble at it . . . Avert the face from it, as the Magi turned, dreading, and, as the symbol, bowed askance . . . "Wonder no longer then, if, rejected so long as an idolatry, the ancient Persians, and their Masters, the Magi — concluding that they saw 'All' in this supernaturally magnificent element — fell down and worshipped it: making of it the physical representation of the very truest, yet, in man's speculation, and in his philosophies — nay, in his commonest reason — impossible God.

And mind you, this is the language, not of a **Parsi** or one of your faith, but of an English scholar who followed the shining path marked out by the Chaldean Magi, and obtained, like them, the true meaning of your mysteries. *Occult Science is the vindicator of Zoroastrianism, and there is none other.* Modern physical science is blind herself to spiritual laws and spiritual phenomena. She cannot guide, being herself in need of a helping hand — the hand of the Occultist and the Hierophant Chaldean sage.

Have you thought *why* the Fire is kept ever burning on your altars? Why is it? Why may not the priest suffer it to go out and rekindle it each morning? Ah! There is a great secret hidden. And why must the flames of one thousand different fires be collected — from the smithy, the burning-kiln, the funeral pyre, the goldsmith's furnace, and every other imaginable source? Why? Because this spiritual element of Fire pervades all nature, is its life and soul, is the cause of the motion of its molecules which produces the phenomenon of physical heat. And the fires from all these thousand hearths are collected, like so many fragments of the universal life, into one sacrificial blaze which shall be as perfectly as possible the complete and collective type of the Light of Ormazd. See the precautions taken to gather only the spirit or quintessence, as it were, of these separate flames. The priest takes not the crude coals from the various hearths and furnaces and pits: but at each flame he lights a bit of sulphur, a ball of cotton, or some other inflammable substance; from this blaze lie ignites a second quantity of fuel; from this a third; from the third a fourth, and so on; taking in some cases a ninth, in others a twentieth flame, until the first grossness of the defilement of the fire in the base use to which it was put has been purged away, and only the purest essence remains. Then only is it fit to be placed on the altar of Ormazd. And even then the flame is not ready to be the type of that Eternal Brightness: it is as yet but a body of earthly flame, a body which lacks its noblest soul. When your forefathers gathered at Sanjan to light the fire for the Indian exiles, the holy Dastur Nairyosang, who had come with them from Persia, gathered his people and the strangers of the country about him in the jungle. Upon a stone block the dried sandalwood is laid. Four priests stand at the four cardinal points. The Gathas are intoned, the priests bow their faces in reverential awe. The Dastur raises his eyes to heaven, he recites the mystical words of power: and lo ! from the upper world of space, descend silvery tongues of flame which lap round the fragrant wood, and it bursts into a blaze. This is the missing spirit evoked by the Adept Prometheus. When *this* is added to the thousand other dancing flames the symbol is perfected, and the face of Ormazd shines before his worshippers. Lighted thus at Sanjan, that historic fire has been kept alive for more than seven hundred years, and, until another Nairyosang appears among you to draw the flames of the ambient ether upon your altar, let it be fed continuously.

This ancient art of drawing fire from heaven was taught in the Samothracian and Kabiric Mysteries. Numa, who introduced the Vestal Mysteries into Rome, thus kindled a fire which was under the care of consecrated Vestal Virgins, whose duty it was, under penalty of death for neglect, to constantly maintain it. It was, as Schweigger shows, the Hermes fire, the Elmesfire of the ancient Germans; the lightening of Cybele; the torch of Apollo; the fire of Pan's altar, the fire-flame of Pluto's helm; the inextinguishable fire in the temple of the Grecian Athene, on the Acropolis of Athens; and the mystical fires of many different worships and symbols. The occult science, of which I spoke, was shared by the Initiates of the Sacred Science all over the ancient world. The knowledge was first gained in Chaldea, and was thence spread through Greece to more western and northern countries. Even today the Fire-cult survives among the rude Indian tribes of Arizona — a far western portion of my native country, America. Major Calhoun, of the U.S. Army, who commanded a surveying party sent out by our government, told me that, in that remote corner of the world, and among those rude people, he found them keeping alight their Sacred Fire in their *teocalis*, or holy enclosures. Every morning their priests go out, dressed in the sacerdotal robes of their forefathers, to salute the rising sun, in the hope that Montezuma, their promised Redeemer and Liberator, will appear. The time of his coming is not foretold, but from generation to generation they wait, and pray, and hope.

In her *Isis Unveiled,* Madame Blavatsky has shown us that this heavenly Fire, however and whenever manifested, is a correlation of the Akasha, and the art of the magician and priest enables him to develop and attract it down. [Occult sound as well as light emanate from 'Akasha': but the true Brahman and Buddhist Initiates make a great distinction between Astral *Fire* and Astral *Light.* Occult sounds and lights are heard and seen by the Yogi, and he *knows* that they proceed from his own *Muladharam* — the first of the six centers of force taught in Yoga philosophy — "The center whose name means the chief foundation or basis is the seat of 'Astral *Fire',*" *they* say.] But to do this he must be absolutely pure — pure in body, in thought, in deed. And these are the three pillars upon which Zoroaster erected the stately edifice of his religion. I have always considered it as a great test of the merit of any religion that its essence can be compressed into a few words that a child can understand. Buddhism, with its noble comprehensiveness, was distilled by its Founder into seven words; Zoroastrianism, is reduced to three — *Humata, Hukhta, Hvarshta.*

A Parsi gentleman, with whom I conversed the other day, explained the fact of your having no wonder-working priests at present by saying that none living were pure enough. He was right, and until you can find such a pure celebrant, your religion will never be again ensouled. An impure man who attempts the magical ceremonies is liable to be made mad or destroyed. This is a scientific necessity. The law of nature, is, you know, that action and reaction are equal. If, therefore, the operator in the Mysteries propels from himself a current of will-power directed against a certain object, and either because of feebleness of will or deviation caused by impure motives, he misses his mark, his current rebounds from the whole body of the Akasha, as the ball rebounds from the wall against which it is thrown to the thrower's hand, and reacts upon himself. Thus, we are told that they who did not know how to manage the miraculous Fire in the Vestal and Kabiric Mysteries "were destroyed by it, and were punished by the Gods". [Ennemoser, *History of Magic,* II, 32] Pliny relates [Histor. Nat, xxviii, 2] that Tullus Hostilius had sought from the books of Numa, "Jovem *devocare a coelo";* but as he did not correctly follow the rules of Numa, he was struck by the lightning. The same rule applies equally to the attempt to use the black art unskillfully. The old English proverb says, "Curses, like chickens, come home to roost". He who would use the powers of sorcery, or black magic, is sure to be destroyed by them first or last. The old fables about sorcerers being carried off by the mocking 'devils' whom, for a time, they had employed to gratify their unlawful desires, are all based upon fact. And, in Zoroastrianism, the Parsi is as carefully taught to eschew and fight against the powers of Ahriman, or the evil Spirits of Darkness, as to cultivate intimacy with and win the protecting favor of the Ameshaspentas and Yazatas — the personified good Principles of Nature. You will not find any of your European authorities speaking of these personifications with decent respect, any more than of the Nature-gods of the Aryans. To their minds these are but the childish fancies of a florid Persian or Aryan imagination, begotten in the infancy of our race, for a good reason, too: not one of these spectacled pandits has the least practical reason to believe that there are such good and evil powers warring about us. But I am not afraid to say to them all in my individual, not official, capacity that I *do* believe in them; nay, that I actually know they exist. And this is why you hear me, a western man taught in a western University and nursed on the traditions of modern civilization, say that Zoroaster knew more about nature than Tyndall does, more about the laws of force than Balfour

Stewart, more about the origin of species than Darwin or Haeckel, more about the human mind and its potentialities than Maudsley or Bain; and so did Buddha and some other ancient proficients in occult science. Pshaw! Young man of the Bombay University, when you have taken your degree, and learned all your professors can teach you, go to the hermit and the recluse of the jungle and ask *him* to prove to you where to begin your real study of the world into which you have been born! Your professors can make you learned but not wise, can teach you about the shell of Nature; but those silent and despised unravellers of the tangled web of existence can evoke for you the soul that lurks within that husk. Three centuries before Christ the United Kingdom of Persia and Media exercised a dominion extending over an area of three or four millions of square miles and had a population of several hundred millions of people. And do you mean to tell me that the Zoroastrian religion could have dominated the minds of this enormous mass of people — nearly twice the present population of India — and could have also swayed the religious thought of the cultured Greeks and Romans, if it had not had a spiritual life in it that its poor remnant of today completely lacks? I tell you that if you could put that ancient life back into it, and if you had your holy men to show this ignorant age the proof of the reality of the old Chaldean wisdom, you would spread your religion all over the world. For the age is spiritually dying for want of a religion that can show just such signs; and for lack of them two crores of western people have become Spiritualists and are following the lead of mediums. And not only *your* religion is soulless. Hinduism, Southern Buddhism, Judaism, and Christianity are so likewise. We see following the missionaries none of the 'signs' that Jesus said should follow those who were really his disciples: they neither raise the dead, nor heal the sick, nor give sight to the blind, nor cast out devils, nor dare they drink any deadly thing in the faith that it will not harm them. There are a few true wonder-workers in our time, but they are among the Lamaists of Tibet, the Copts of Egypt, the Sufis and Dervishes of Arabia and other Muhammadan countries. The great body of the people in all countries, has become so sensual, so avaricious, so materialistic and faithless, that the moral atmosphere is like a pestilential wind to the Yozdathraigar (those Adepts whom we have made known to India under the name of BROTHERS).

The meaning of your Haoma you doubtless know. In the ninth Yaçna of the Avesta, Haoma is spoken of both as a God — Yazata — and as the plant or juice of the plant, which is under his especial protection; and so is the Soma of the *Aitareya Brahmana*.

At the time of morning-dawn came
Haoma to Zoroaster,
As he was purifying the fire and reciting the Gathas. Zoroaster asked him:
Who, O man, art thou?
Thou, who appearest to me as the most beautiful in the whole corporeal world, endued with thine own life, majestic and immortal?
Then answered me Haoma, the pure, who is far from death. Ask me, thou Pure one, make me ready for food.
Thus in the same line, is Haoma spoken of in his personified form and as a plant to be prepared for food. Farther on he is described as
Victorious, golden, with moist stalks.

This is the sacred Soma of the Aryans — by them also elevated into a deity. This is that wondrous juice which lifted the mind of him who quaffed it to the splendors of the highest heavens, and made him commune with the Gods. It was not stupefying like opium, not maddening like the Indian hemp, but exhilarating, illuminating, the begetter of divine visions. It was given to the candidate in the Mysteries, and drunk with solemn ceremonies by the Hierophant, Its ancient use is still kept in your memories by the

Mobeds drinking in the Yacna ceremony, a decoction of dried Haoma stalks, that have been pounded with bits of pomegranate root in a mortar and afterwards had water thrice poured over them.

The Beresma twigs — among you represented by a bunch of brass wires — are a reminiscence of the- divining-rods anciently used by all practitioners of ceremonial magic. The rod or staff was also given to the fabled gods of Mythology. In the fifth book of the *Odyssey,* Jupiter, in the Council of the Gods, bids Hermes to go upon a certain mission, and the verse says:

> *Forth sped he ....*
> *Then taking his staff, with which he the eyelids of mortals Closes at will, and the sleeper, at will, re-awakens.*

The rod of Hermes was a magic staff; so was that of Aesculapius, the healing wand that had power over disease. The Bible has many references to the magic rod, notably in the story of the contest of Moses with the Egyptian Magicians in the presence of Pharaoh; in that of the magical budding of Aaron's rod; and in the laying of Elisha's staff on the face of the dead Shunamite boy. The Hindu Gossain of our day carries with him a bamboo rod having seven knots or joints, that has been given to him by his Guru and contains the concentrated magnetic will-power of the Guru. All magic-rods should be hollow, that the magnetic power may be stored in them. In the Yacna II., note that the priest, holding the Baresma rods in his hand repeats constantly the words, 'I wish' — properly, I will — so and so. By the ceremony of concentration of the sacred twigs a magical power has been imparted to them, and with the help of this to fortify his own will-force, the celebrant seeks the attainment of his several good desires: the heavenly Fire, the good Spirits, all good influences throughout several kingdoms of

Nature, and the Law or WORD. In the middle ages of Europe, divining-rods were in general use, not only to discover subterranean waters and springs, and veins of metal, but also fugitive thieves and murderers. I could devote an entire lecture to this subject and prove to you that this phenomenon is a strictly scientific one. In Baring-Gould's *Curious Myths of the Middle Ages* will be found highly interesting accounts of these trials of the mystical power of the rods which time forbids my quoting. To this day the rods are employed to discover springs, and the Cornish miners carry sprigs of hazel or other wood in their caps. The author of the work named, while ascribing the strange results he is obliged to record principally to the imagination, is yet constrained to add that, "The powers of Nature are so mysterious and inscrutable that we must be cautious in limiting them, under abnormal conditions, to the ordinary laws of experience". And in this he is backed up by the experience of many generations of witnesses, in many different countries.

We have mentioned the invocation of the divine Word or Name in the Yacna. All the ancient authorities affirm that there is a certain Word of Power by pronouncing which the Adept subjugates all the forces of Nature to his will. It is mentioned by many authors. One of the latest is the author of a book called *Rabbi Jeshua,* who, speaking of Jesus, says, " He had perhaps endeavored to employ magic arts, and to bewitch the Council by invocation of the Name through which all incantations were rendered effective" [p. 143] Among the Aryans, the Agnihotra priest used to prepare the sacrificial wood and, upon reciting the appropriate Mantra, the heavenly fire of Agni would descend and kindle it. In the Avesta, Zoroaster smites the fiends with the spiritual power of the Word. [Darmesteter, lxxvii] It represents him as a saint militant, repelling force by force. In Fargard xi, Zoroaster asks Ahura-Mazda how he shall purge the house, the fire, the water, the earth, the cow, the tree, the faithful man and woman, the stars, the moon, the sun, the boundless light, and all good things.

Ahura Mazda answers:

Thou shalt chant the cleansing words, and the house shall be clean, clean shall be the fire, etc.

So thou shalt say these fiend-smiting and most healing words; thou shalt chant the Ahunavairya five times, etc..

Then are given various words to employ for different acts of cleansing. But the WORD the one most potent — the Name which Proclus in his treatise upon the Chaldean Oracles says, "rushes into the infinite worlds", is not written there. [Though properly — the Word or the NAME is neither a word nor a name in the sense we give it] Nor can it be written, nor is it ever pronounced above the breath, nor, indeed, is its nature known except to the highest Initiates. The efficacy of all words used as charms and spells lies in what the Aryans call the Vach, a certain latent power resident in Akasha. Physically we may describe it as the power to set up certain measured vibrations, not in the grosser atmospheric particles, whose undulations beget light, sound, heat and electricity, but in the latent Spiritual Principle or Force about the nature of which modern science knows scarcely anything. No words whatever have the slightest efficacy unless uttered by one who is perfectly free from all weakening doubt or hesitancy; who is for the moment wholly absorbed in the thought of uttering them; and has a cultivated power of will which makes him send out from himself a conquering impulse. Spoken prayer is in fact an incantation, and when spoken by the heart as well as by the lips, has a power to attract good and repel bad influences. But to patter off prayers so many times a day while your thoughts are roving over your landed estates, fumbling your money-bags, or straying away among any other worldly things, is but mere waste of breath. The Bible says: "The prayer of the righteous availeth much"; and so it does. There is the case of George Muller, of Bristol, England, who for thirty years has supported the entire expenses of his orphanage — now a very large institution of charity — by the voluntary gifts of unknown passers-by at the door, who drop into his charity boxes the exact sum he prays for to meet the day's necessities. History does not contain a more curious or striking example than this. This man prays with such faith and fervency, his motives are so pure, his labors so beneficent, that he attracts to him all the good influences of Nature, although he knows neither the 'Ahunavairya,' nor Aryan mantras, nor the Buddhistic Pirit. Use what words you may, if the heart is clean, the thought intense, and the will concentrated, the powers of Nature will come at your bidding and be your slaves. The Dabistan says. [P.2]

Having the heart in the body full of Thy remembrance, the novice, as well as the Adept, in contemplation

Becomes a supreme king of beatitude, and the throne of the kingdom of gladness. Whatever road I took, it joined the street which leads to Thee;

The desire to know Thy being is also the life of the meditators;

He who found that there is nothing but Thee has found the final knowledge

The Mobed is the teacher of Thy truth, and the world a school.

But this Mobed was not a mere errand-runner, or droner of Gathas perfunctorily without understanding a word he was saying, but a real Mobed. So high an ideal of human perfectibility had he to live up to, that Cambyses is said to have commanded the execution of a priest who had allowed himself to be bribed; and had his skin stretched over the chair in which his son and successor sat in his judicial capacity. [History *of Magic,* I. 2] Mobed is derived from Mogbed — from the Persian *Mog,* and means a true priest. Ennemoser truly says that the renowned wisdom of the Magi in Persia, Media, and the neighboring countries, "contained also the secret teachings of philosophy and the sciences, which were only communicated to priests, who were regarded as mediators between God and man, and as such, and *on account of their knowledge,* were highly respected."[Ibid] The priests of a people are exactly what the people require them to be. Remember that, friends, and blame yourselves only for the state of religion among you. You have just what you are entitled to. If you yourselves were more pure, more spiritual and more religious, your priesthood would be so. You are merchants, not idolaters, but — as Professor Monier William pithily remarks in the *Nineteenth Century* (March 1881) — worshippers of the solid rupee. The genuine Parsi, he says, "turns with disgust from the hideous idolatry practiced by his Hindu fellow-subjects. He offers no homage to blocks of wood and stone, to monstrous many-headed images, grotesque symbols of good luck, or four- armed deities of fortune. But he bows down before the silver image which Victoria the Empress of India, has set up in her Indian dominions".

And this, according to Zoroastrianism, is a crime as great. In his ecstatic vision of the symbolical scenes shown him by the angel Serosh-Yazata for the warning and encouragement of his people, Ardai Viraf, the purest of Magician Priests at the court of Ardeshir Babagan, saw the pitiable state to which the soul of a covetous miser is reduced after death. The poor wretch, penniless — since he could take not a *dime* with him — his heart buried with his savagely-loved treasures, his once pure nature corrupted and deformed — moved the Seer to profoundest pity. "I saw it" says he, "creep along in fear and trembling, and presently a wind came sweeping along, loaded with the most pestilential vapors, even as it were from the boundaries of hell .... In the midst of this wind appeared a form of the most demoniacal appearance .... The terrified soul attempts to escape but in vain; the awful vengeful shape by voice and power roots him to the spot. He enquires in trembling accents who it may be, and is answered: "I am your genius" (that is, his spiritual counterpart and now his mastering destiny) " and have become thus deformed by your crimes; whilst you were innocent I was handsome. ... You have laid in no provisions for this long journey; you were rich but did no good with your riches ... and not only did no good yourself, but prevented, by your evil example, those whose inclinations led them to do good; and you have often mentally said, 'When is the day of judgment? To me it will never arrive' ". [Ardai *Viraf, Nameh,* by Captain J. A. Pope, p 56] Say it is a vision, if you will, yet nevertheless it mirrors an awful truth. The worship of the silver image of Victoria on the Rupee is even more degrading than the Hindu's worship of Ganesha or Hari; for he, at least, is animated by a pious thought, whereas the greedy money-getter is but defiling himself with the filth of selfishness.

The Parsi community is already half-way along the road to apostacy. Gone is the fiery enthusiasm that made your forefathers give up everything they prized rather than repudiate their faith; that supported them during a whole century in the sterile mountains of Khurasan or the outlying deserts; that comforted them in their exile at Sanjan, and gave them hope after the battle with their hereditary enemy Aluf Khan. Formerly, it was religion first and Rupee last; now it is Rupee first and everything else after it. See! I, a stranger, point with one finger to your palatial bungalows, your gorgeous equipages, and your ostentatious annual squandering of twelve lakhs of money at festivals; with the other to the wretched subscription of Rs. 16,000 towards the support of Rahannmai Mazdiyasna Sabha — a good society for the promotion of your religion among your own children, and of Rs. 10,000 to the orthodox Parsi Society of Khetwadi! The proverb says, "Figures cannot lie", and in this instance they did not. If I wanted the best test to apply to your religious zeal, I should look at the sum of your expenditures for vain show and sensual enjoyment, as compared with what you do for the maintenance of your religion in its purity; and to the sort of conduct you tolerate in your priests. That is the mirror that impartial justice holds up before you; behold your own image, and converse with your conscience in your private moments ! What but conscience is personified in the "maid of divine beauty or fiendish ugliness", according as the soul that approaches the Chinvad bridge was good or bad in life? [Yasht xxii] "She the well-shapen, strong and tall-formed maid, with the dogs at her sides, one who *can distinguish* . .. and is of *high understanding"*. [Vendidad, Fargard xix]

You have asked me to tell you about the spirit of your religion. I have only the truth to tell — the exact truth, without fear or favor. And I repeat, you are already half-way towards religious repudiation. You have already set money in the niche of faith; it only remains for you to throw the latter out of doors. For hypocrisy will not last for ever. Men weary of paying even lip-service to a religion they no longer respect. You can deceive yourselves, you cannot deceive that maiden at the bridge. Let three or four more generations of skeptics be passed through the educational mint of the college; and let the teaching of your religion be neglected as it now is; and the time will have come when it will be only the occasional brave heart that will dare call himself a Mazdean. Let that stand as a prophecy if you choose: it *is* one, and it is based upon the experience of the human race. A black page will it be indeed, in the record of human events, when the last vestiges of the once splendid faith of Zoroaster shall be blotted from it, the last spark of the heavenly fire that shone from the Chaldean watch-towers of the Sages be extinguished. And the more so, when that last extinction shall be caused, not by the sword of tyranny nor by the crafty scheming of civil administrators, but by the worldliness of its own hereditary custodians; those to whom the lighted torch had been handed down through the ages, and who dropped it into the quenching black waters of Materialism.

Time fails me to enter into detailed explanation of the Zoroastrian symbols as perhaps I might — though I certainly am not able to do the subject full justice. The sudra and kusti with which you invest your children at the age of six years and three months have of course a magical significance. They pass through the hands of the Dastur who as we have seen was formerly an Initiate, and he imparted to them magnetic properties which converted them into talismans against evil influences. After that a set formula of prayers and incantations is regularly prescribed for the whole life. The wearer's thoughts are directed towards the talismanic objects constantly and, when the faith is present, his or her will-power, or magnetic aura, is at such time infused into them. This is the secret of all talismans; the object worn, whatever it may be, need have no innate protective property, for that can be given to any rag, or stone, or bit of paper, by an Adept. Those of you who have read the Christian Bible will remember that from the body of Paul the Apostle, "were brought unto the sick handkerchiefs or aprons, and the diseases departed from them, and the *evil spirits went out of them*". [Acts xix, 12] In the Ahuramazda-Yasht of the Khordeh-Avesta, it is written "by day and night, standing or sitting, sitting, or standing, girt with the Aiwyaonhana (kusti) or drawing off the Aiwyaonhana.

> *Going forwards out of the house, going forwards out of the confederacy, going forwards out of the region, coming into a region.*
>
> *Such a man the points of the Drukhs-souled, proceeding from Aêshma, will not injure in that day or that night, not the slings, not the arrows, not knives, not clubs; the missiles will not penetrate and he be injured. [Haug's Avesta, p 24, Khordeh-Avesta, English Edition of 1864]*

Similar protective talismans are given by every Adept to each new pupil.

The use of Nirang for libations and ablutions is a survival of very ancient — probably pre-Iranian — mythic conceptions. There is nothing in the fluid itself of a disinfectant or purificatory character, but a magical property is given to it by ceremonial magical formulas, as a glass of common water may be converted into a valuable medicine by a mesmeriser, holding it in his left hand and making circular passes over it with his right.

"The storm floods that cleanse the sky of the dark fiends in it were described in a class of myths as the urine of a gigantic animal in the heavens. As the floods from the bull above drive away the fiend from the god, so they do from man here below; they make him ' free from the death-demon' (franasu), and the death fiend flies away hell-wards, pursued by the fiend-smiting spell: ' Perish Thou, 0 Drug . . . never more to give over to Death the living world of the good Spirit' ". [Nineteenth Century, January, 1881, p 176]. It may be that there is a more valid reason for the use of Nirang, but I have not yet discovered it. That an occult property is imparted to the fluid by the ceremonial is clear, since if it be exposed to certain influences not in themselves putrefactive it will speedily become putrid; while, on the other hand it may be kept for years in a fresh condition without the admixture of antiseptic substances, and notwithstanding its occasional exposure to the air, if certain ceremonial rules be followed. (Of course I have this from Parsi friends and not from my own observation. I would not express an unqualified opinion before investigating the subject.) I recommend some Parsi chemist to analyze specimens of different ages, especially to determine the relative quantities of nitrogenous constituents.

The subject is treated in Darmesteter's 'Introduction' to the *Vendidad*.

When Professor Monier Williams vents his Oxonian scorn upon the ceremonies of the Parsis he thereby only provokes the pity of such as have looked deeper than he into the meaning of ancient symbolism. "Here and there" says he, "lofty conceptions of the Deity, deep philosophical thoughts and a pure morality are discoverable in the Avesta like green spots in the desert; *but they are more than neutralized by the silly puerilities and degrading superstitious ideas* which crop up as plentifully in its pages as thorns and thistles in a wilderness of sand" [lxxxviii]. Mr. Joseph Cook, the other day in this hall, said the same. The good portions of the Vedas were, he said, so few as compared with the trashy residuum, that he likened them to the fabled jewel in the head of a filthy toad. It is really very kind of these white Pandits to admit that there is anything whatever except rottennes and puerility in the old religions. Give each a statue!

In what has been said I have, you must remember, been speaking from the standpoint of a Parsi. I have tried to sink my personality and my personal religious preferences for the moment and put myself in your place. That is the cardinal policy of the Theosophical Society. It has itself no sectarian basis, but its motto is the Universal Brotherhood of man. It was organized to bring to light the long buried truths of not one, but of all the world's archaic religions. Its members are of all respectable castes, all faiths and races. It has many intelligent Parsis among them. For the sake of them and their co-religionists, this lecture has been given. I have tried most earnestly to induce one of them or some other Parsi to come forward and show you that no religion has profounder truths, deeper spiritual truths, concealed under its familiar mask, than yours. That I am the incompetent though willing spokesman for the ancient Yozdathraigar is your fault, not mine. If I have spoken truth, if I have suggested new thoughts, if I have given any encouragement to the pious or pleasure to the learned, my reward is ample.

"Yatha Ahu Vairyo": "The Riches of Vohumano shall be given to him who works in this world for Mazda ..." is the promise of the Avesta [Fargard xxi] Bear it in mind, ye Mazdeans, and remember the maiden and her dogs by the Chinvad Bridge. I say this especially to my Parsi Brothers in our Society, for I have the right to speak to them as an elder to his junior. As Parsis they have a paramount duty to their co-religionists, who are retrograding morally for want of the pure light. As Theosophists their interest embraces all their fellowmen of whatever creed. For we read in one of the most valuable of all the books for the thoughtful Parsi the *Dabistan or School of Manners:*

> *The world is a book full of knowledge and of justice, The binder of which book is destiny, and the binding the beginning and the end; The future of it is the law, and the leaves are the religions persuasions . . .*

For three years we have been preaching this idea of mutual toleration and Universal Brotherhood here in Bombay. Some have listened, but more have turned a deaf ear. Nay, they have done worse — they have spread lies and calumnies about us, until we were made to appear to you in a false light. But the tide is turning at last, and public sympathy is slowly rising in our favor. It has been a dark night for us; it is now sunrise. If you can see a good motive behind us and an honest purpose to do good by spreading truth will you not join us, as you have other societies, and help to make us strong. We can perhaps be of service in aiding you to learn something more than you know about the spirit of Zoroastrianism. As I said before, there are many important secrets to be extracted from ancient MSS. in Armenia. Perhaps they may be got at if you will join together and send some thoroughly competent Parsi scholars to make the search in co-operation with the Tiflis Archaeological Society. See how the Christians have organized a Palestine Exploration Society to search for anything in the shape of proof that can be found to corroborate their Bible. For years they have kept engineers and archaeologists at work. Is your religion less important to you? Or do you mean to sit on your guineas until the last old MSS. has been burnt to kindle Armenian fires or torn to wrap medicines and sweets in, as I have seen Bibles utilized in India and Ceylon by heathen Borahs? One of our members [See *The Theosophist,* July, 1881] went over the most important ground a few months ago. At the monastery of Soorb Ovanness in Armenia there were in 1877 three superannuated priests: now there remains but one. The "library of books and old manuscripts heaped up as waste paper in every corner of the pillar-cells, tempting no Kurd, are scattered over the rooms", he says; and, "For the consideration of a dagger and a few silver *abazes* I got several precious manuscripts from him" (the old priest). Now does not this suggest to you that through the friendly intermediation of our Society, and the help of Madame Blavatsky, you may be able to secure exceptional advantages in the matter of archaeological and philosophical research connected with Zoroastrianism? We do not ask you to join us for our benefit, but for your own. I have thrown out the idea; act upon it or not as you choose. Beaten with Parsi children's shoes ought the Parsi to be who next gives a gaudy nautch or wedding tamasha unless he has previously subscribed as liberally as his means allow to a fund for the promotion of his religion.

I told you in commencing that this subject of the spirit of Zoroastrianism is limitless. In consulting my authorities I have been perplexed to choose from the abundance of material, rather than troubled by any lack of it. There are a few more facts that I would like to mention before closing.

Abul Pharaj, in the *Book of Dynasties* [ii, p 54] states that Zoroaster taught the Persians the manifestation of the Wisdom (the Lord's Anointed Son, or Logos,, the Persian ' Honovar '). This is the living manifested Word of deific Wisdom. He predicted that a Virgin should conceive immaculately, and that at the birth of that future messenger a six-pointed star would appear and shine at noon-day. In its center would appear the figure of a Virgin. This six pointed star you see engraved on the seal of the Theosophical Society. In the Kabalah the Virgin is the Astral Light or Akasha and the six pointed star the emblem of the macrocosm. The Logos or Sosiosh to be born means the secret knowledge or science which reveals the 'Wisdom of God'. Into the hand of the Prophet Messenger, Zoroaster, were delivered many gifts. The act of filling the censer with *fire from the sacred altar,* as the Mobed did in ancient days, was symbolical of *imparting to the worshippers,* the knowledge of divine truth. In the *Gita,* Krshna informs Arjuna that God is in the fire of the altar. "I am the Fire; I am the Sacrifice". The Flamens, or Etruscan priests, were so called because they were supposed to be illuminated by the *tongues of Fire* (Holy Ghost) and the Christians took the hint. [Acts. ii.] The scarlet robe of the Roman Catholic cardinal symbolizes the heavenly Fire. In an ancient Irish MSS. Zoroaster is called *Airgiod-Lamh* or he of the Golden Hand — the hand which received and scattered celestial fire. [Ousley's *Oriental Collections,* I 303] He is also called Mogh Naudhat, the Magus of the new ordinance, or dispensation. Zoroaster was one of the first reformers who taught the people a portion of that which he had learned at his initiation, namely, the six periods or *gahambars* in the successive evolution of the world. The first is *Maedyozarem,* that in which the heavenly canopy was formed; the second, *Maedyoshahem,* in which the collected moisture formed the steamy clouds from which the waters were finally precipitated; the third, *Paetishahem* when the earth became consolidated out of primeval cosmic atoms, the fourth, *Iyathrem* in which earth gave birth to vegetation; the fifth, *Maediyarem* when the latter slowly evolved into animal life; the sixth, *Hames-pithamaedem,* when the lower animals culminated in man. The seventh period — to come at the end of a certain cycle — is prefigured in the promised coming of the Persian Messiah, seated on a horse: when the sun of our solar system will be extinguished and the 'pralaya' will begin. In the Christian *Apocalypse* of St. John you will find the Persian symbolical prophecy closely copied; and the Aryan Hindu awaits the coming of his Kalaki Avatar, when the celestial White Horse will come in the heavens, bestridden by Vishnu. The horses of the Sun figure in all other religions.

There exists among the Persian Parsis a volume older than the present Zoroastrian writings. Its title is *Javidan Khirad,* or Eternal Wisdom. It is a work on the practical philosophy of Magic, with natural explanations. Hyde mentions it in his preface to the *Religo Veterum Persarum.* The four Zoroastrian 'Ages' are the four races of men — the black, the russet, the yellow, the white. The four castes of Manu are alleged to have typified this, and the Chinese show the same idea in their four orders of priests clothed in black, red, yellow and white robes. St. John sees these same colors in the symbolic horses of his *Revelation.* Speaking of Zoroaster, whom he admits as having possessed knowledge of all the sciences and philosophy then in the world, the Rev. Oliver gives an account of the cave temple of which so much is said in Zoroastrian literature. "Zoroaster", he writes, "retired to a *circular* cave or grotto in the mountains of Bokhara which he ornamented with a profusion of symbolical and astronomical decorations, consecrating it to Methr-Az. . . . Here the sun was represented by a splendid gem . . . in a conspicuous part of the roof . . . and the four ages of the world were represented by so many globes of gold, silver, brass and iron. [History of Initiation, p 9]

And now gentlemen — orthodox and heterodox — leaders among the Parsi community — a word with you on practical matters before we part. In three days more I shall leave Bombay on a long journey and the accidents of travel, to which we are all liable, may prevent my ever addressing you again. I pray you therefore, to listen to what a sincere friend has to say, a friend who is none the less one in that he never asked you for a piece of your money for himself, and never will.

I have lived among you for three years. During this time I have been associating on terms of confidential intimacy with some of your most intelligent young men. I have admitted them and, in some cases, their wives with them, into our Society. Thus I have perhaps had exceptional opportunities to learn the real state of your people and religion. I find both in sore need of an organized, unselfish and persistent effort among yourselves. Your people look up to you as their best advisers, the Mobeds respect your influence and court your favor. You have it in your power to do a world of good. Will you do it? You now spend annually from twelve to fifteen lakhs of rupees upon stupid *tamashas* — that do not belong to your own religion at all; that give you no real pleasure; that crush many poorer than you to the very ground with debt; that defile your own natures with disgusting pride and conceit; that encourage intemperate habits in the young and that weaken pious inclinations. The burden of these upon the community is so sore, and the common-sense of your best men so revolts at them, that years ago you would have returned to the simpler pleasure of your forefathers, had you not lacked the moral courage to combine. A reform like this is never to be effected individually; the leaders must combine. Take two of the fifteen lakhs you now worse than waste and put it aside as a Fund for the promotion of the Mazdean Religion and see what you might do for your children and children's children. Do not tell me you cannot afford to create such a Fund, when the whole world knows that you are ready to give thousands to every object suggested by a European for the benefit or flattery of some one of his race and even to rear statues to those who are not the friends of your religion. "Charity begins at home"; give, then, first to your own people, and of your remaining surplus to outside objects.

There is a fatal inactivity growing apace among you. Not only are you not the religionists you were; you are not the old-time merchants. You are being elbowed out of commerce, and it is not very uncommon to see your sons going from door to door in search of employment at salaries of from fifty to seventy-five rupees per month, with their pockets full of Matriculation papers or F.E.A. and B.A. diplomas. And instead of your being as in the olden time, the kings of Indian trade and commerce, you are jostled by successful Bhattias, Borahs, Maimans, and Kkojahs who have accumulated fortunes. You are making no proper effort to impart a practical knowledge of your religious principles and tenets to the educated rising generation; hence very naturally they are largely becoming skeptics and infidels. They do not as yet actually despise their religion *en masse* — the time for that has not quite arrived; but, on account of your neglect to show them its sublimity and make them deeply respect it, they have reached the stage of indifference. One necessary step would be to have your prayer-books translated into the Vernacular and English, with footnotes to explain the text and especially commentaries to show the reconciliation of Mazdean philosophy with modern science. It is worse than useless — it is highly injurious to one's faith — to patter off prayers in an unknown tongue, encouraging the hypocrisy of pretending to be pious while one has not the food at hand for a single pious thought. I have watched both Priests and Behedin at their prayers, morning and evening and seen more that were not attending to the business in hand than that were.

If you wish to revive your religion, you should, besides organizing the exploring expeditions and archaeological surveys I previously spoke of, also rear a class of Parsi preachers who would be able to expound, it thoroughly and maintain it against all critics and enemies. These men should be highly educated and versed in Samskrt, Zend, Pahalvi, Persian and English.. Some should know German and French — like my honored friend Mr. Kama. With western literature they should be familiar. Some should be taught oratory so as to expound in a popular style the sacred theme. It might also be well to found travelling scholarships, as the Europeans have, to be given to especially meritorious students.

A stricter moral example should be set by you to your youth, who have, as I said above, fallen in too many cases into evil ways. They do not regard truth, nor show as much respect to elders, as formerly.

As your understanding of the Spirit of your religion has decreased, you have been growing more and more superstitious; essentials are neglected, and non-essentials given an exaggerated consequence.

Finally, and chiefly, the priestly class needs a thorough reformation. There are more than you need to perform the offices of religion, and the profession being over-crowded, their influence is continually decreasing and they have come, as a Parsi gentleman once remarked to me, to be looked upon as licensed beggars — a state of things which must certainly grieve your really learned Dasturs more than any one else.

The foregoing thoughts are submitted to you with great deference and in the hope that they will be pardoned in view of the kindly interest which prompts them. Before embodying them in this discourse I have taken the counsel of one of my most respected Parsi friends, so that you may regard them as in fact the views of one of your own community.

And now I ask you, as a final word, if the crisis has not arrived when each of you is called upon, for the sake of all he holds sacred, to be up and doing. Shall the voice of Chaldean Fathers, which whispers to you across the ages, be heard in vain? Shall the example of Zoroaster and others be forgotten? Must the memory of your hero-forefathers be dishonored? Shall there never more arise among you a Dastur Nairyosang Dhaval to draw down the celestial flame from the azure vault upon your Temple-altar? Is the favor of Ahura-Mazda no longer a boon precious enough to strive for and to deserve? The Hindu pilgrims to the Temple-shrine of the Jotir Math at Badrinath affirm that some, more favored than the Test, have sometimes seen far up amid the snow and ice of Mount Davalagiri, a Himalayan peak, the venerable figures of Mahatmas — perhaps of Rshis — who keep their ward and watch over the fallen Aryan faith and wait the time for its resuscitation. So too our Brother travelling in Armenia writes: "there is a cave up near the crest of Allah-Dag, [A mountain chain of Great Armenia. For particulars of the legend here described see *The Theosophist*, Vol II, p 213] where at each setting of the sun, appears at the cave's mouth a stately figure holding a book of records in his hands". The people say that this is Mathan, last of the great Magian priests; whose body died some sixteen centuries ago. His anxious shade watches from thence the fate of Zoroaster's faith. And shall he stand in vain? Is he to see that faith die out for want of spiritual refreshment? Ye sons of Sohrab and of Rustam, rouse! Awake ere it is too late! The hour is here; where are the MEN?

www.ingramcontent.com/pod-product-compliance
Lightning Source LLC
LaVergne TN
LVHW041501070426
835507LV00009B/744